ACHIEVEMENT DUET SHEETS

Chinese Dragons

by
NANCY FABER

I. Dragon Dance

II. Dragon's Gate (Sacred to Dragons)

III. Dragons in the Clouds

Chinese Dragons

Dragons have a rich, mythical history in China. According to legend, thousands of dragons live in the pools, rivers, and Chinese seas. Contrary to dragons of Western mythology, Chinese dragons do not breathe fire, fiercely eat people, or have wings, though they are able to fly. Chinese dragons fly up into the clouds and play in the summertime, then return to the rivers and pools where they sleep during winter.

Ancient Chinese myth tells us that rivers and streams were carved out of the land by the powerful tail of the dragon. When cutting the course of the Yellow River, a famous dragon named Yu lashed through rocky cliffs forming a great chasm. This place was called *Dragon's Gate* and became sacred to dragons.

FABER
PIANO ADVENTURES®

EXCLUSIVELY DISTRIBUTED BY

HAL•LEONARD®

Commissioned by the 2000 Goshen College Piano Workshop

Chinese Dragons

I. Dragon Dance

Secondo

Nancy Faber

Commissioned by the 2000 Goshen College Piano Workshop

Chinese Dragons

I. Dragon Dance

Primo

Nancy Faber

AD3005

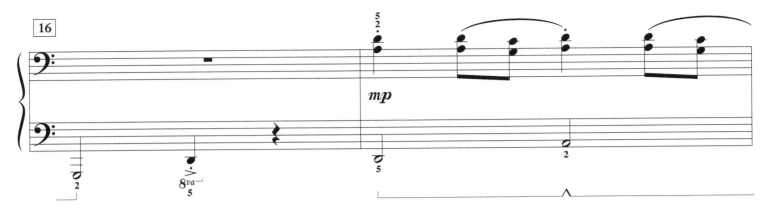

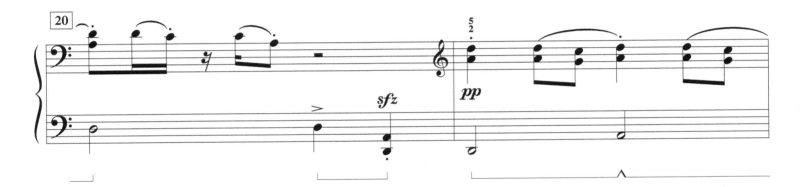

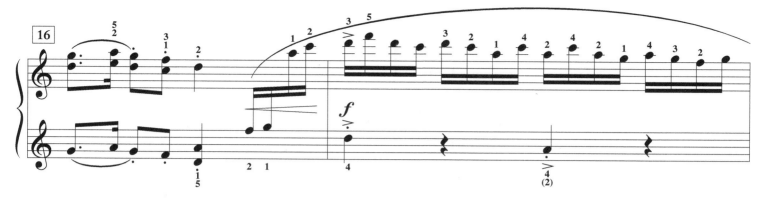

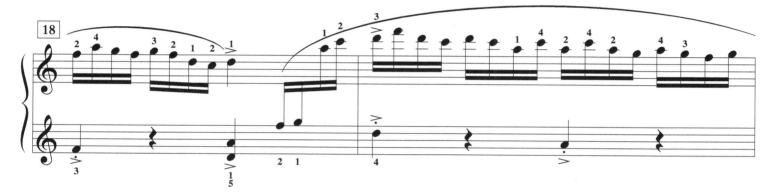

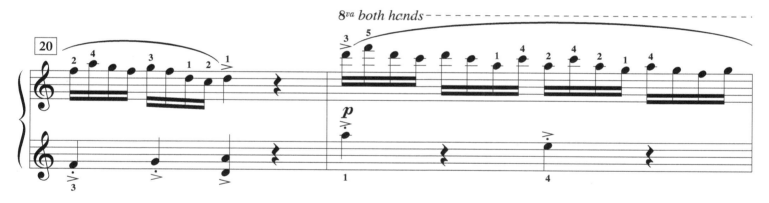

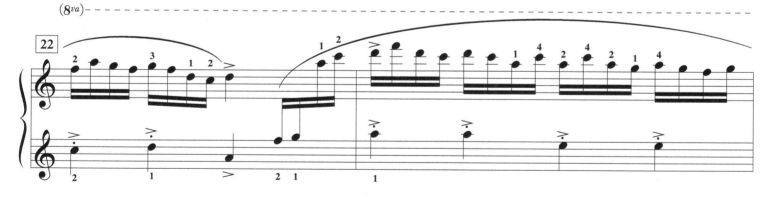

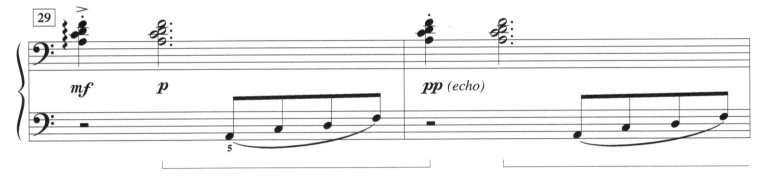

Grandioso, meno mosso (♩ = ca. 92)

Tempo I (Allegro)

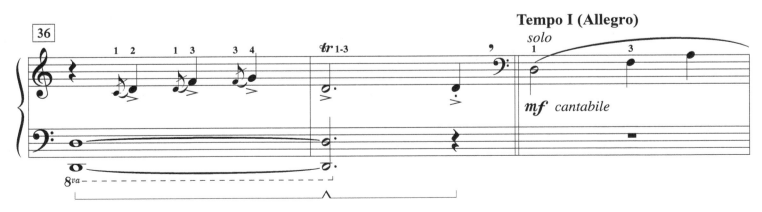

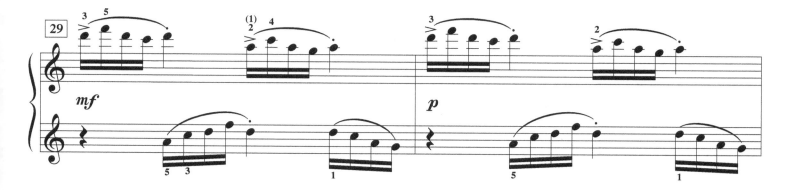

Grandioso, meno mosso (♩ = ca. 92)

Tempo I (Allegro)

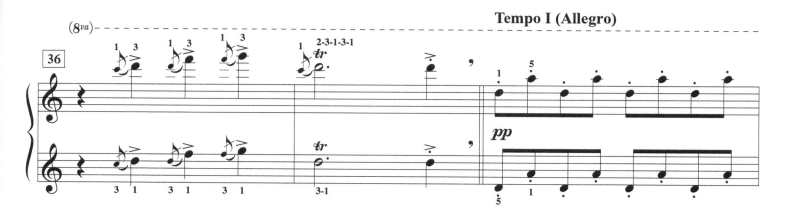

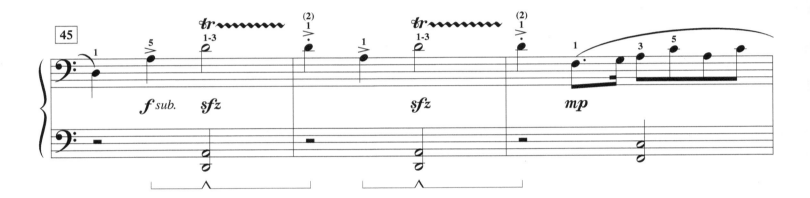

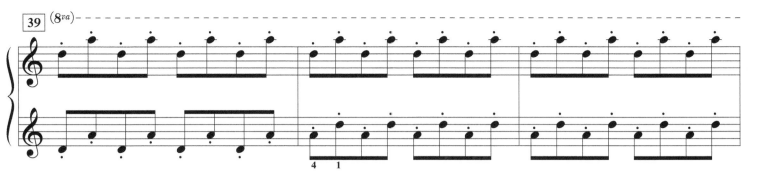

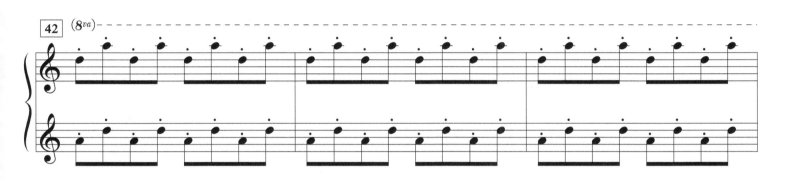

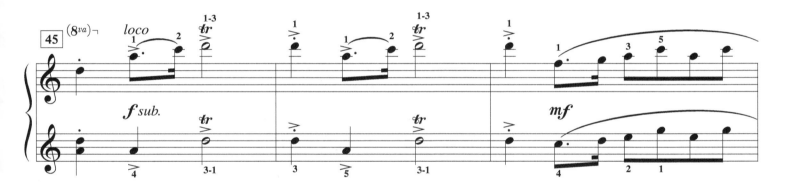

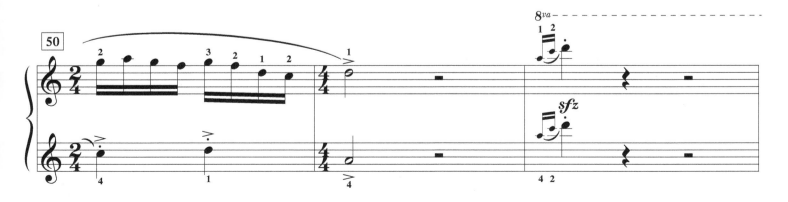

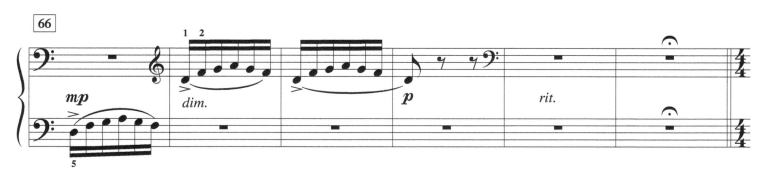

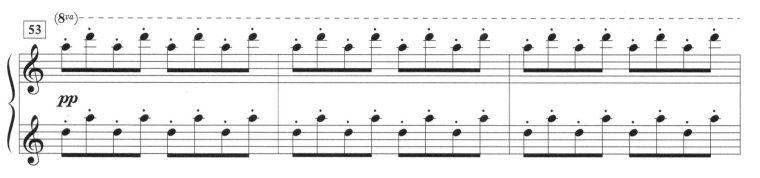

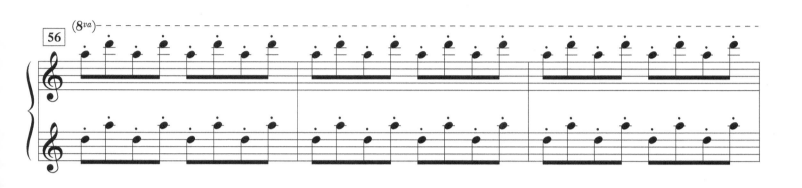

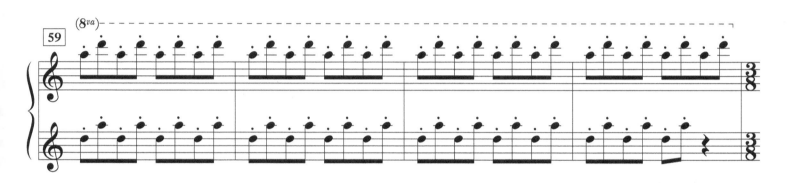

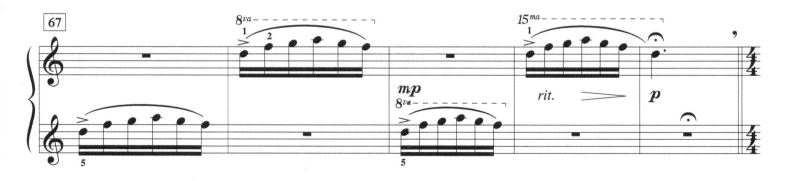

Secondo

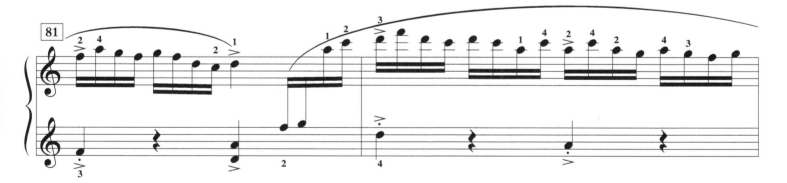

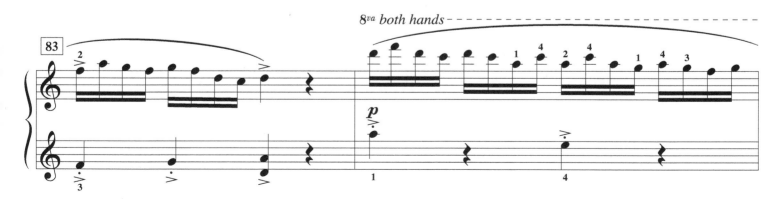

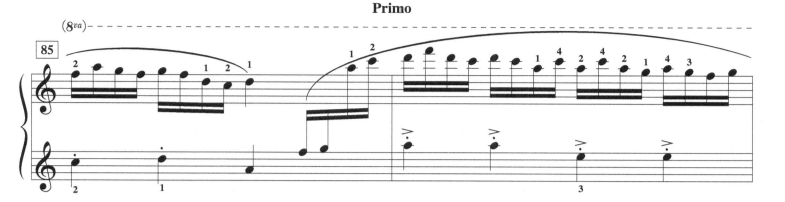

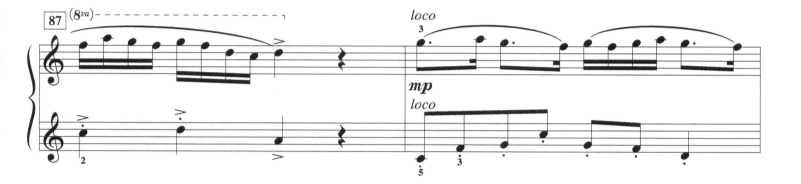

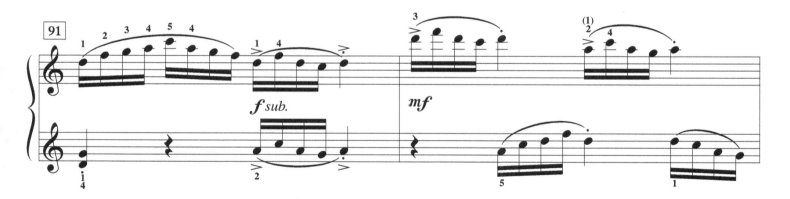

Grandioso, meno mosso (♩ = ca. 92)

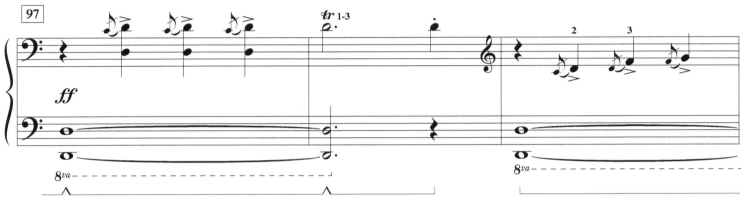

Tempo I (Allegro)

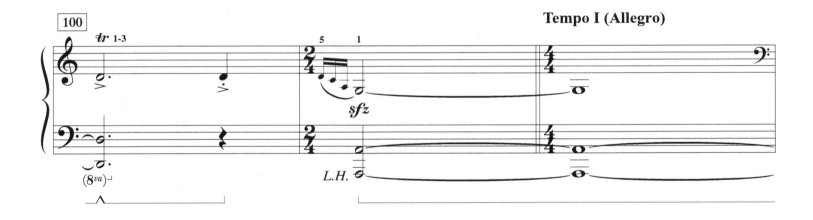

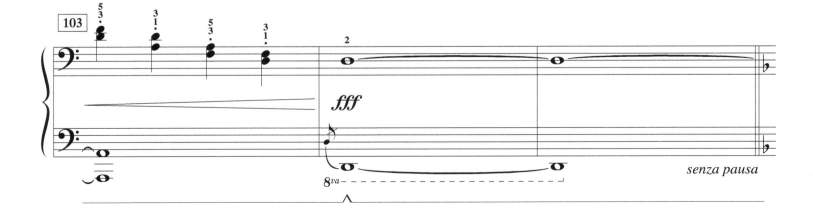

senza pausa

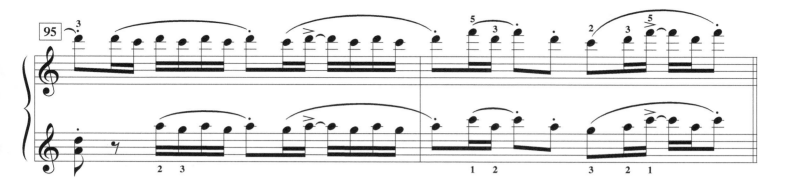

Grandioso, meno mosso (♩ = ca. 92)

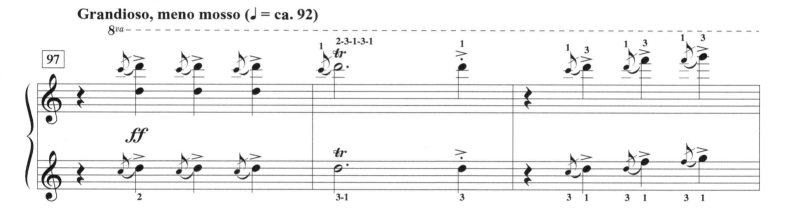

Tempo I (Allegro)

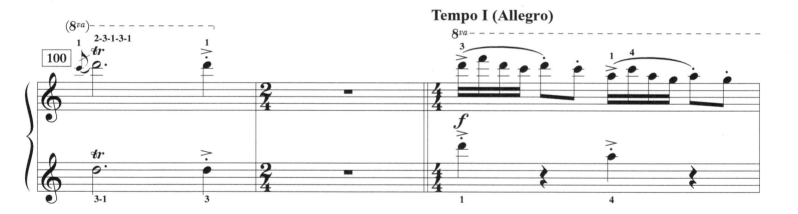

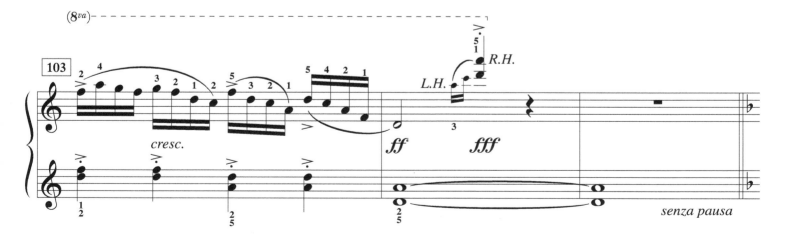

senza pausa

II. Dragon's Gate
(Sacred to Dragons)

II. Dragon's Gate
(Sacred to Dragons)

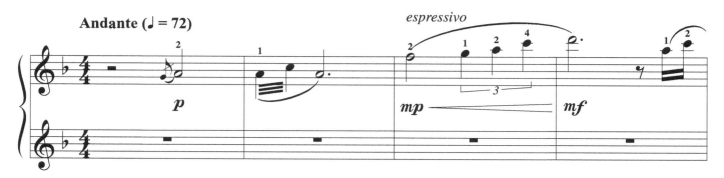

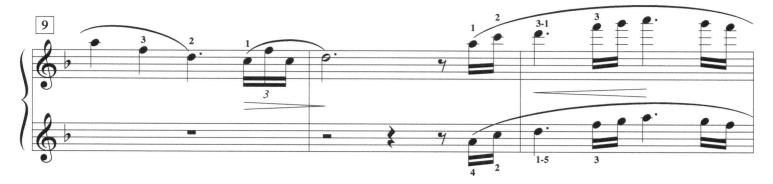

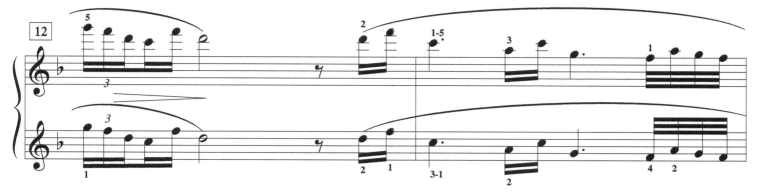

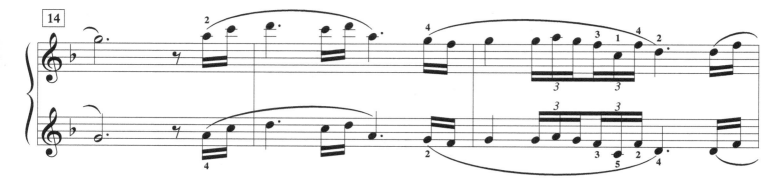

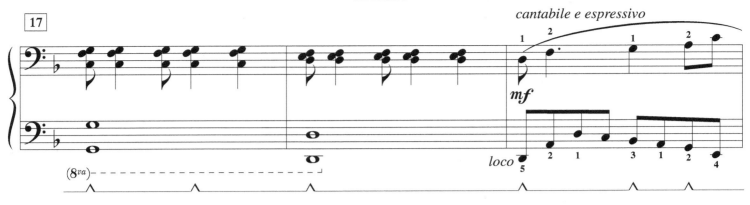

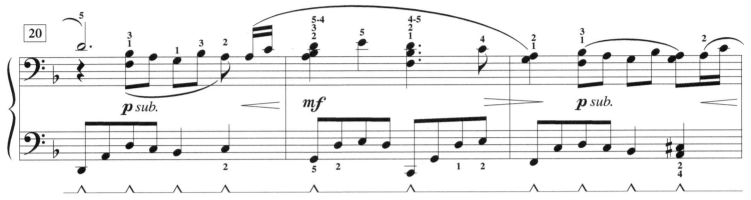

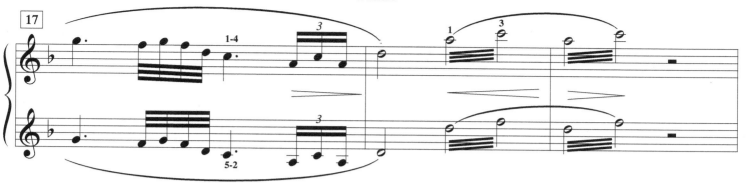

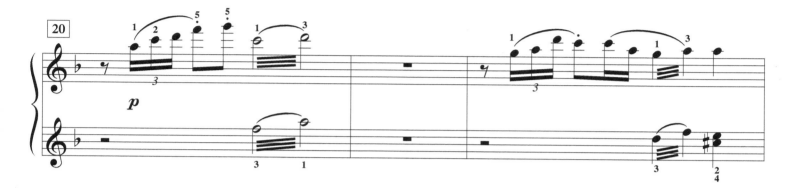

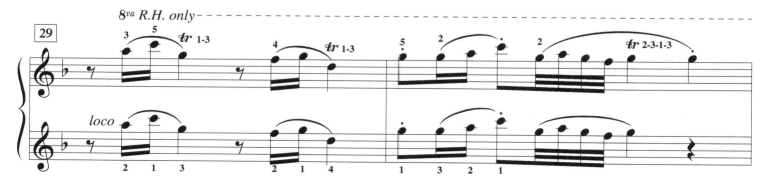

Secondo

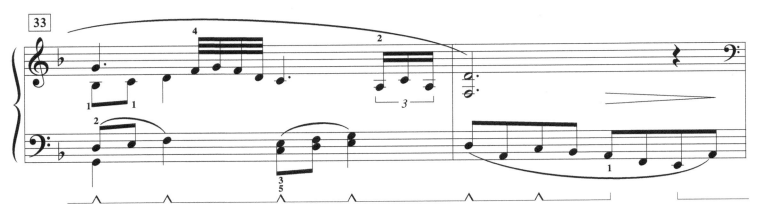
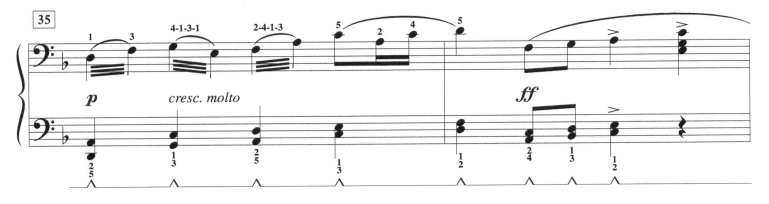

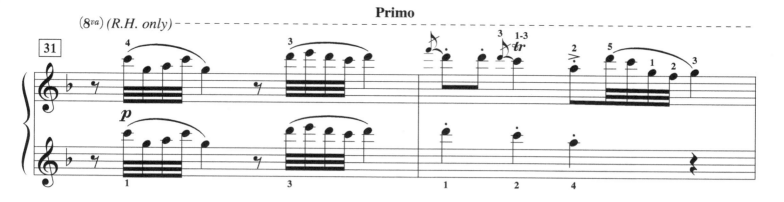

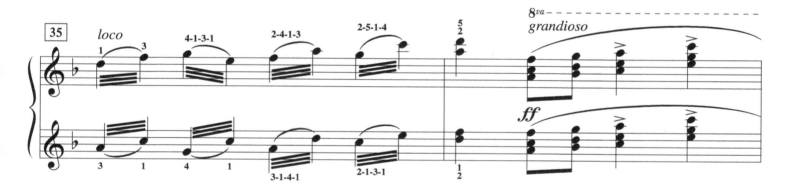

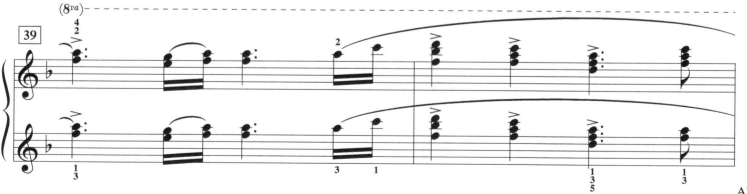

AD3005

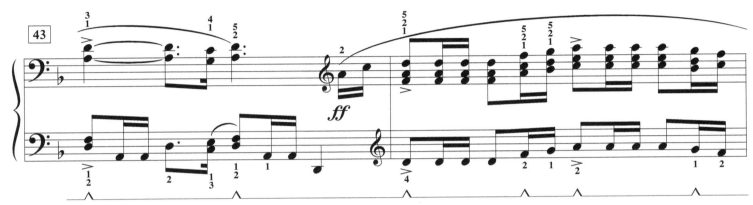

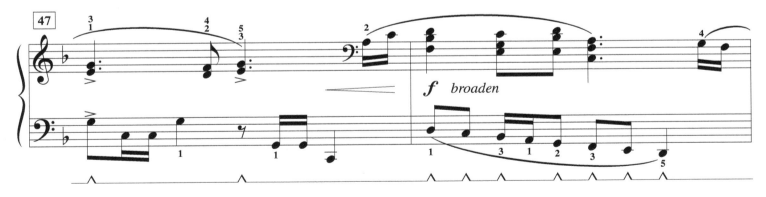

Primo

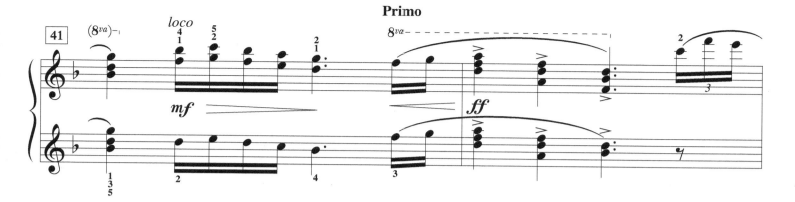

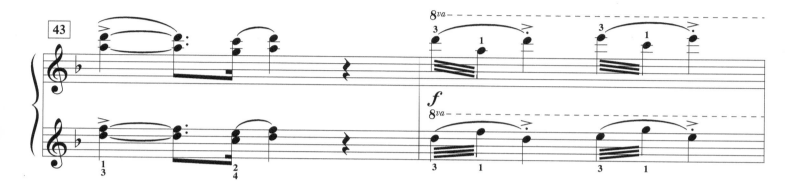

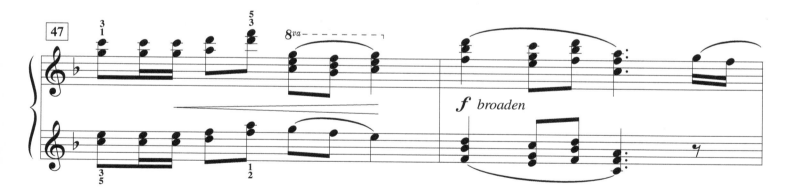

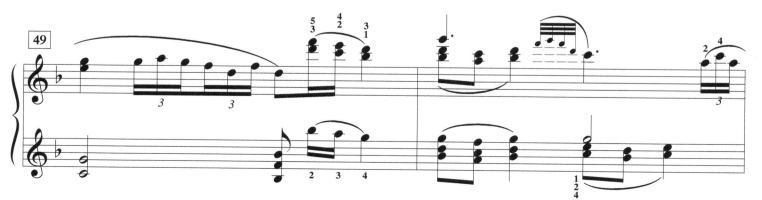

Secondo

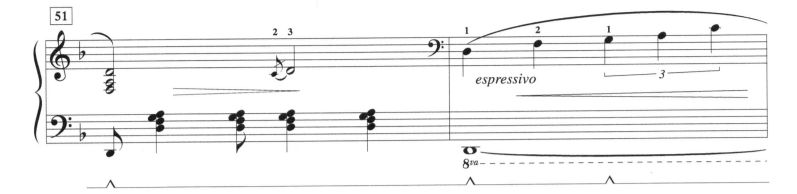

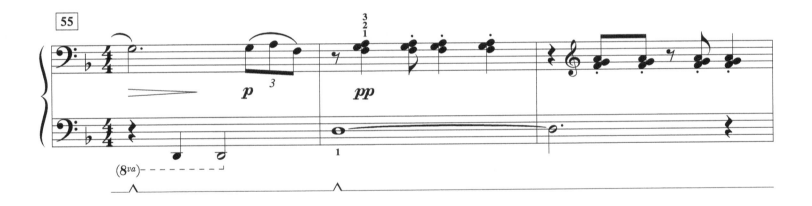

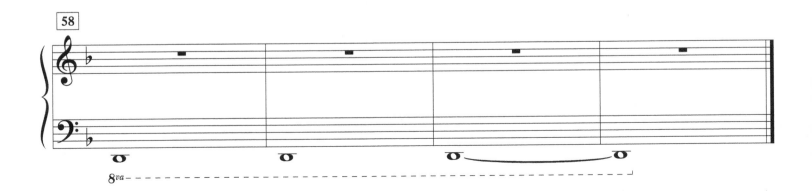

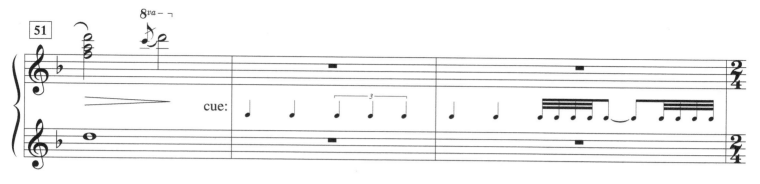

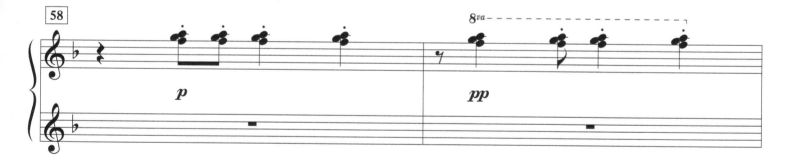

III. Dragons in the Clouds

Vivace (♩ = 138)

III. Dragons in the Clouds

Vivace (♩ = 138)

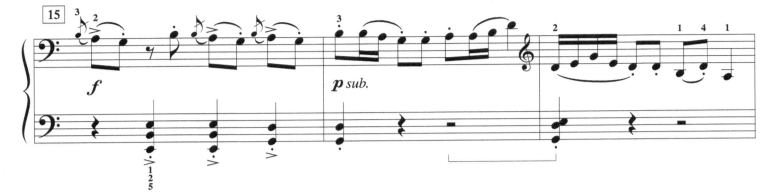

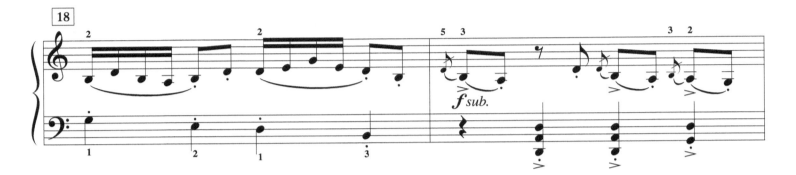

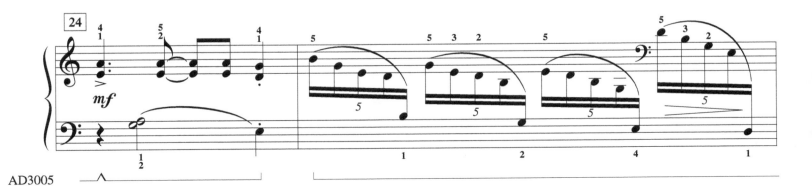

Primo

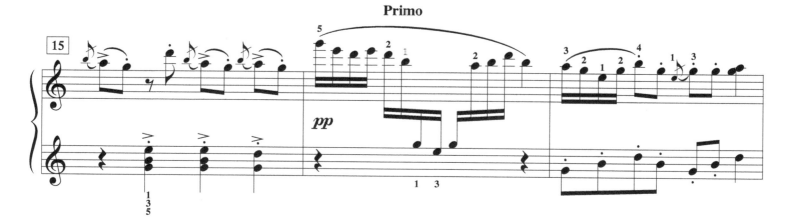

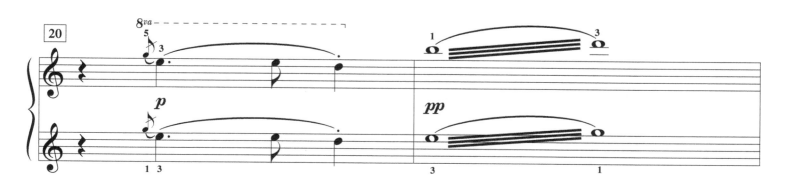

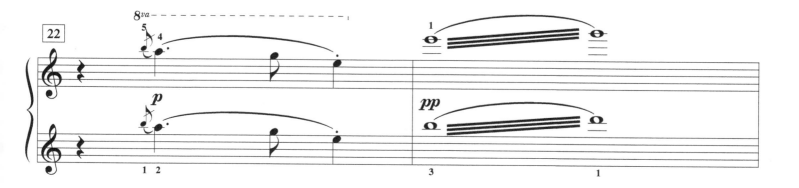

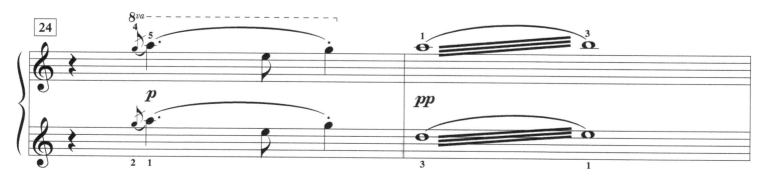

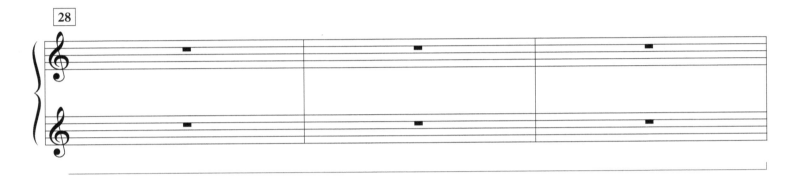

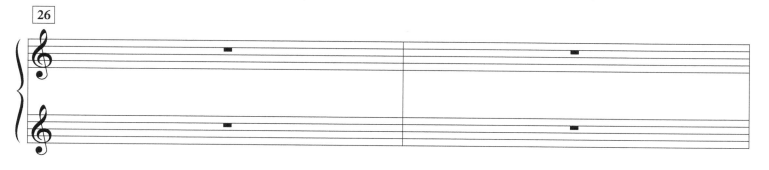

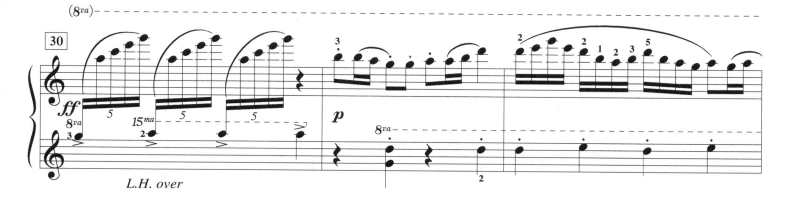

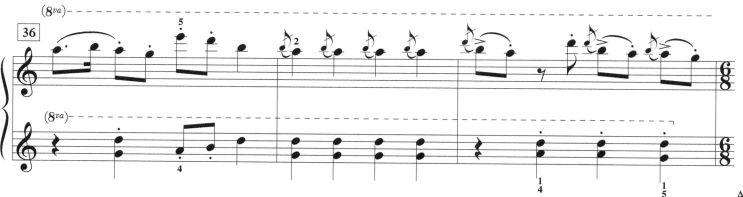

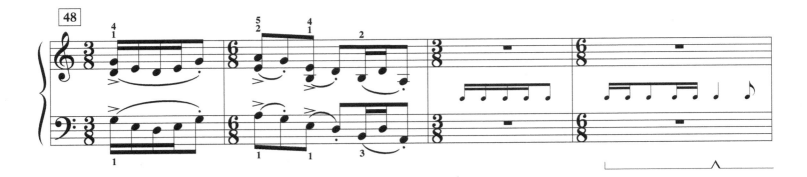

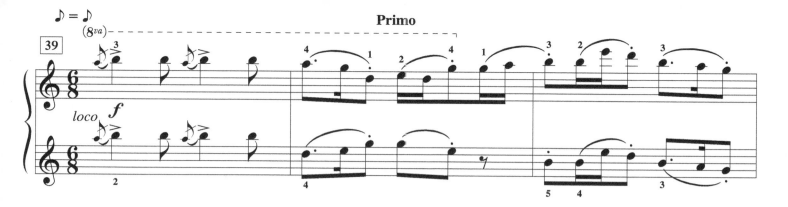

Primo

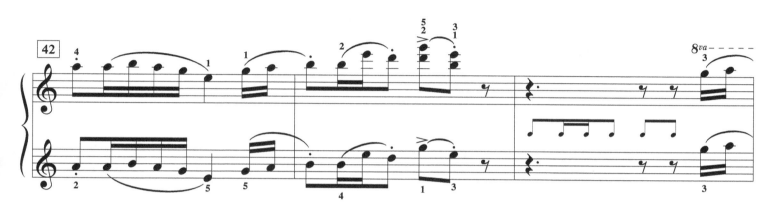

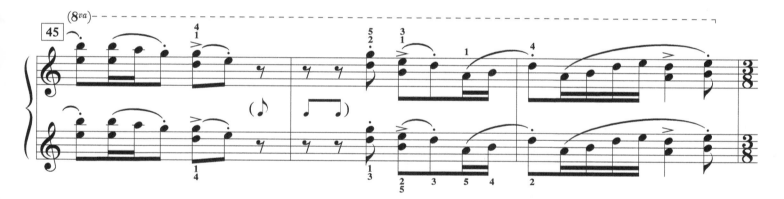

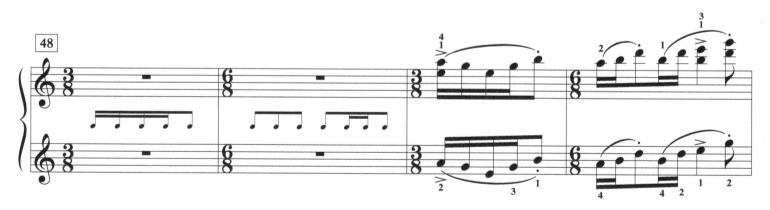

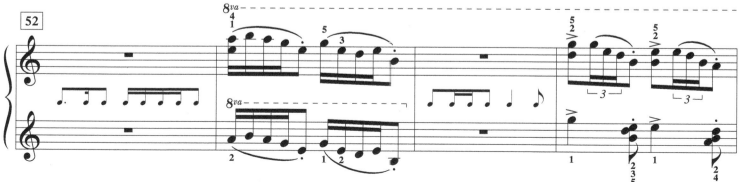

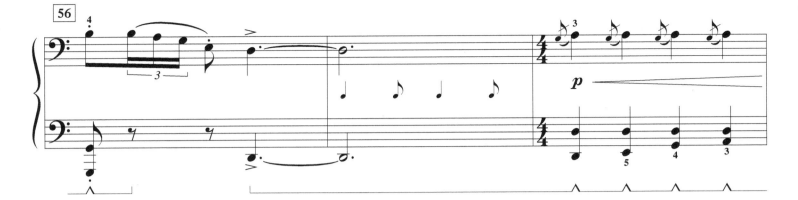

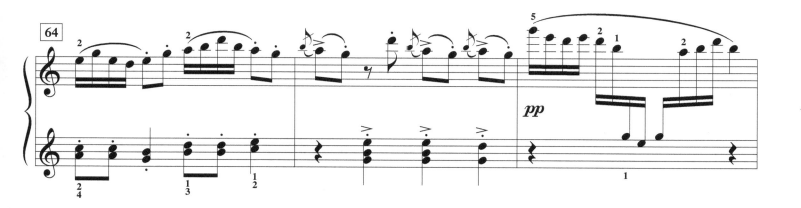

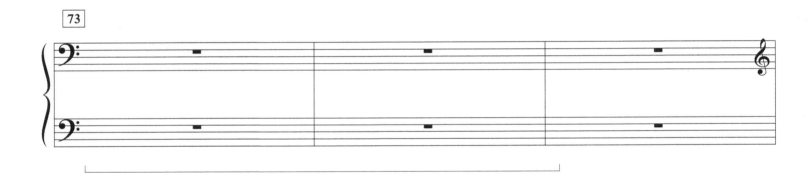

Broadly

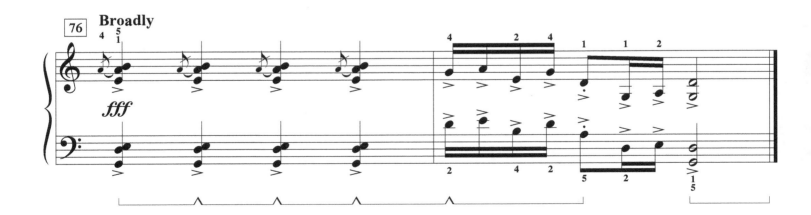

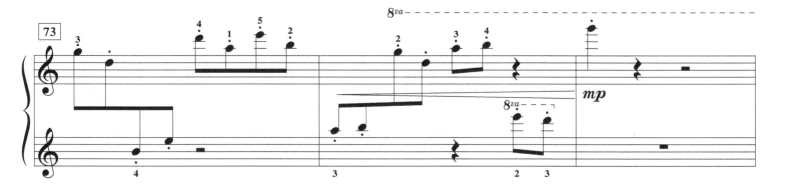

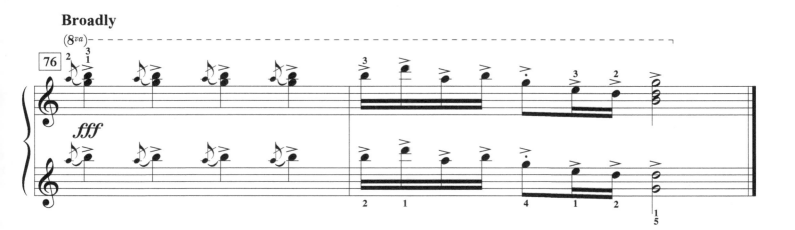